KNOW YOUR CANARIES SERIE.

THE
GLOSTER
CANARY

OTHER TITLES AVAILABLE
(or in production)

Canary Standards in Colour
G. T. Dodwell
Special Edition with 32 colour plates of canaries extra.
ready for framing and de-luxe binding

Canary Breeding for Beginners
James Blake

The Fife Canary
T. Kelly and James Blake (limp)

The Gloster Canary
James Blake (limp)

The Norwich Canary
K. W. Grigg and James Blake (limp)

The Roller Canary
Revised by George Preskey (limp)

The Yorkshire Canary
Ernest Howson (hardback)

The Yorkshire Canary
Shackleton (limp) Reprint of Classic

THE
GLOSTER
CANARY

by

James Blake

Beech Publishing House
Station Yard
Elsted
Midhurst
West Sussex GU29 0JT

ISBN 1-85736-151-2

First published in 1988.
Reprinted 1989
Second Edition 1997

BLC -in Publication Data
A catalogue record for this book is available
from the British Library

Beech Publishing House
Station Yard
Elsted
Midhurst
West Sussex GU29 0JT

CONTENTS

Correction
*Chapters 5 to 8 in the text are shown as 13
to16, but should be as given above.*

INTRODUCTION

Canaries are popular throughout the world and have been for centuries. Their colour, "personalities" and song have provided enjoyment to their owners and from Victorian times they have been exhibited and bred to conform with the standards laid down by the specialist canary clubs and societies.

That a species of bird should be bred in such a variety of shapes and colours is a marvel in itself. If recorded stories are true canaries have shown talents way beyond what might be imagined possible.

There have been cases of a whistling canary who was self-taught to mimic a bullfinch and there was the famous talking canary who was able to utter such sentences as "Sweet pretty dear", "Sweet Pretty Queen" and could even imitate the ringing of a bell and the grating of a wire.

A witness to the prowess of the bird wrote a poem which is reproduced below:

Thou wert surely more than bird,
  Little golden-winged Canary!
That of late I sweetly heard
  Speaking like a tiny fairy

Aye, a fairy sure thou wert,
  Who, a gilded plume and feather
(Just to give thy spirit mirth.)
  Did'st assume, then hasten'd hither.

For thy silver bits of speech
  For thy tunes and tones delicious—
Ladies left their harps and lutes,
  Thee to hear and see, ambitious!

So, for many a day and week,
  Thou did'st most perplex and worry
Thinking men, who heard thee speak—
  Speech correct enough for Murray.

Thus thy little fairy-sprite,
  Did delight to play and chatter,
While the puzzled wits of men
  Scarce could comprehend the matter.

But at last, of that same sport
  All a-weary grew thy spirit,
And again it sighed and pined
  Fairy regions to revisit.

Therefore 'twas thou threw'st aside
  Guise assumed and shape Canary,
And, clad in elfin pride,
  Sought again the realms of fairy.

In Tudor times in England and in the seventeenth century in Holland canaries were regarded as symbols of wealth and elaborate cages were used to house them.

AVIARIES

Large aviaries were built to house canaries and other birds. It is recorded that Charles II created Birdcage Walk in London by hanging cages and their occupants for all to enjoy. In Victorian times large aviaries, almost house-like were produced to accommodate their feathered friends.

In the Victorian fashion the birds were objects of sentiment. They went to great lengths and around 1880 it was recorded in *Familiar Friends* by Olive Patch (Cassell, London) as follows:

When we were at Felixstowe last Summer, we saw a curious collection of performing birds. They were canaries that had been trained to draw a little coach, outside of which sat another as coachman, whilst a fourth stood up behind as footman. Another carried a couple of pails across its shoulders just like a milkman. But the most wonderful of all were a bullfinch and a sparrow. The bullfinch had a little gun which he fired off at the sparrow, when the latter would drop as if it had been shot, although of course he was not hurt in the least.

The drawing made at the time is reproduced below:

Performing Birds

The utility aspects of canaries should not be forgotten. Until quite recently canaries were used extensively in the mines for detecting carbon monoxide gases. Where possible danger exists the miners advance along the roadways in the mine with the canaries in small cages and at the first sign of gas the birds succumbs and are then withdrawn — usually to be revived in the fresh air. Around 2000 canaries are kept in aviaries for this purpose, but they are being phased out by the use of electronic equipment which apparently is not as popular as the canaries to the miners who generally love all birds and to which they become attached.

Canaries continue to be kept and bred in considerable numbers. They provide a focus of interest for those who wish to relax and enjoy their management including breeding, rearing and showing. This book attempts to show how best to keep them and to enjoy their presence to the full

. ACKNOWLEDGEMENTS

We acknowledge the assistance given by various individuals, companies and organisations who assisted in the writing of this book. A list of commercial businesses is given in an Appendix and it is hoped that its inclusion will show fanciers some of the sources of equipment. It is not fully comprehensive, nor is the fact that a name is included as a guarantee of quality but we certainly found them responsive to enquiries which is a good sign.

Inevitably many fanciers, clubs and societies were consulted and our thanks are offered to those who responded with help and advice. In particular:

1. Mrs Tamson Waller for a number of the drawings of canaries and plants.
2. *Cage and Aviary Birds* Editorial Staff.
3. Ron and Val Moat for photographs of Gloster and Fife Canaries.
4. Various fanciers who supplied information or photographs and other experiences with their own birds.
5. A.J. Mobbs author who supplied a number of photographs on aspects of bird breeding.

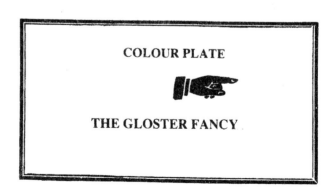

COLOUR PLATE

THE GLOSTER FANCY

Gloster Fancy Canaries – Clear Consort and Variegated Corona

1
INTRODUCING
THE
GLOSTER CANARY

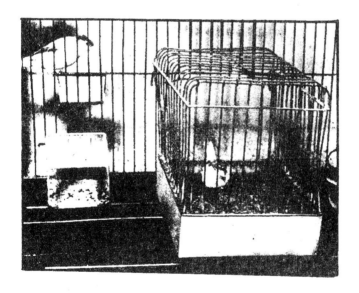

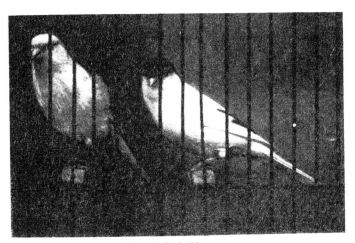

Fig. 1-0 Early Glosters

A.W. Smith regarded these as a well matched pair of birds — A Buff Consort cock and a White Corona hen — that would produce Whites and Normals.

HISTORY

The Gloster Canary is a relatively new canary first seen and acknowledged as a separate breed in 1925. It exists in two forms:

1. **Crested** (known as the Corona)
2. **Plainhead** (termed the Consort)

The male or female may be either type, but for breeding it must always be **Corona x Consort.**

Although the emphasis tends to be on the Corona, both types are essential. The Consort must have a well-shaped head or the progeny will not comply with the *standards*.

TYPE

The Gloster is a small bird with a full body which is well rounded. The emphasis is on **diminutive;** i.e. tiny.

In later Chapters more details are given on type, and faults which may be found. There are also drawings and photographs illustrating how the breeder may recognise a typical Gloster.

STANDARDS

Standards are laid down by the Gloster Canary Convention. They are broken down as follows:

		Points
1.	**CORONA,** i.e. Crest	15 + 5 for definite centre
2.	**HEAD OF CONSORT**	15 + 5 for Browiness
3.	**BODY**	20
4.	**TAIL**	5
5.	**CARRIAGE**	10
6.	**LEGS AND FEET**	5
7.	**SIZE** (Smallness)	15
8.	**PLUMAGE**	15
9.	**CONDITION**	10
		100

Corona neat, round regular.

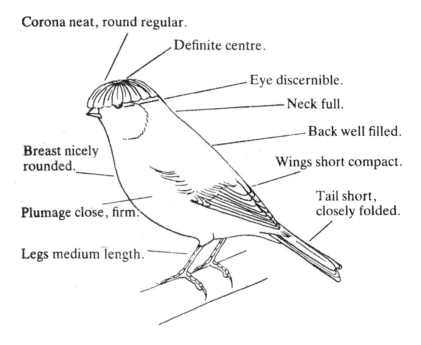

Definite centre.

Eye discernible.

Neck full.

Back well filled.

Breast nicely rounded.

Wings short compact.

Plumage close, firm.

Tail short, closely folded.

Legs medium length.

Figure 1-1 Points of a Gloster Canary From Canary Standards in Colour (G. T. Dodwell)

It will be seen that except for the head the *standards* are the same for both types.

MAIN FEATURES

1. DIMINUTIVE

A tiny bird of cobby stature is called for and any which show coarseness or oversize should be penalised.

2. ROUNDED BODY

A short, cobby Bird well balanced should be the aim. Those with long thin bodies are not representative of the breed.

3. CREST OR HEAD

In the **Corona** the crest should be **round, neat** and **regular** — essential descriptions. Moreover, the eye should be visible which means the crest should not be too long. There should be no faults in the crest.

With the **Consort** a well rounded head is essential and this should not appear too wide, although the *standard* does state the eyebrow should be heavy and show brow. However, the latter should not be excessive.

4. PLUMAGE

Great store is set on fine, good quality plumage. It should be close, rather like the quality known to poultry fanciers as "hard feathered". Colour is not critical, but should be a good "natural colour". Green, cinnamon, white and buff are all to be found. In addition, the crests may be in different colours and light bodied birds with dark crests are greatly admired.

5. CARRIAGE

The description "Carriage" in the *Standard* does not refer to **posture,** but to the alertness and activity of the bird. The stance should be about 45° which looks natural when viewing the bird (see Figure 1.1) Any tendency to be upright or lean over the perch should be penalised.

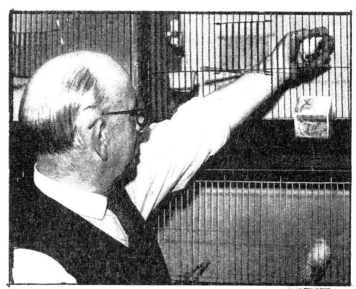

Figure 1-2 A.W. Smith, the Pioneer largely responsible for establishing the Gloster Canary. Demonstrating how to handle a bird — vital for its training.

Figure 1-3 A Gloster Buff Corona showing a compact body (Photo: Ron and Val Moat)

2

HISTORY OF THE CANARY

8

Figure 2-1 The Wild Canary

EARLY ORIGINS

The canary in its wild state came from the Canary Islands which is situated off the north-west coast of Africa. It belongs to the Finch family which nests in orange trees growing along the banks of streams. The climate in the Canary Islands is warm and equable.

In colour the wild canary is greyish green or grass green with darker tail and coverts. The natural colour is greyish brown on the shoulders, and back with the lower parts a lighter, yellow colour. Their legs and beak are quite dark and, according to the Rev. Francis Smith, they are "stunning black" with a stout and powerful body.

As a song bird the wild canary is also subdued. The warbling resembles that of the linnet or bullfinch and does not reach the magnificence of the domesticated canary. The reason is that the latter has been bred for fancy points, including its singing qualities, which have been cultivated over many generations.

INTRODUCTION INTO EUROPE

The most widely held belief appears to be that canaries were introduced into Europe in the Sixteenth century. They came from Italy having settled in Elba when a ship bound to Leghorn became shipwrecked and birds on board escaped.

This event has been described by a number of earlier writers and an excellent summary is provided by G.J. Barnesby *(The Canary)*:

A ship, which, in addition to other merchandise, had a multitude of Canaries on board that were consiged to Leghorn, was wrecked on the coast of Italy, and the birds which thereby obtained their liberty, flew to the nearest land. This happened to be Elba, where they found so propitious a climate that they multiplied without the intervention of man, and would probably have naturalised themselves had not the wish to possess them been so great as to occasion their being hunted after till they were entirely extirpated. In Italy, therefore, we find the first tame Canaries, and they are still reared there in great multitudes. At first their rearing was attended with considerable difficulty, partly because the mode of treating these delicate strangers was not sufficiently understood, and partly because the males chiefly, and not the females, were brought to Europe. There is much difference in appearance of plumage compared to that of the birds said to be of the original stock. Darwin's supposed natural law of selection, climate, domestication, and food, may have tended to bring forth specimens now so different in colour to the Canary of past ages. The birds, subsequent to their domestication in Belgium, Germany, and England, it is asserted, threw up small patches of lighter or yellow feathers, and the breeders, by carefully matching those birds that bore the largest number, succeeded in obtaining bright and uniform colour more resembling those of the present date.

EARLY PUBLICATIONS

Early mentions of canaries which allow the fancier to see the special interest displayed in the species are summarized below:

1. Conrad Gesner

The author refered to the canary as the "sugar bird". His book on the natural history of birds was published in 1555.

2. Aldrovarus

A famous writer, he described the canary, explaining that they descended from the Canary Islands as described in a different part of this chapter.

3. Samuel Pepys

In his *Diary* on 11th January 1665, Pepys recorded distress because his canary bird had died. It will be appreciated that this event was in the reign of Charles II!

4. Gent

Gent a writer on animal husbandry wrote in 1675, that canaries were quite popular in Germany and to a lesser extent in Britain.

5. Hervieux 1709

Hervieux a Frenchman was the author of a comprehensive book on canaries.(published 1709). He stated that canaries were bred throughout Europe and there were many varieties. At this date attention was being paid to the colour of the bird as well as its song.

As quoted, in the early days, the emphasis was on develping song birds without regard for shape, type, colour or other characteristic. Since then the many varieties have evolved and, with the exception of the roller canary, the exhibition characteristics developed have been on the "fancy points" relating to size, conformation and colour.

Colour Canaries †

Various mutations have appeared over the period when canaries have been bred in domestication. Examples are as follows.*

1. Whites (available from 1677)

These were produced by accident from a genetic change in the characteristics of the birds being bred from. They apparently died out and reappeared after a period of almost 200 years when a Miss Lee of Martinborough, New Zealand bred a White canary in 1908 and another in London the same year bred by W. Kiesel.

---

* **From an article *Colour Breeding in Canaries* A.K. Gill, Cage Bird Annual, 1939. The author was a pioneer in Colour Canary breeding.**
† **Not to be confused with the feeding of colour food to some breeds.**

2. Cinnamons which appeared some time prior to 1709, but, again, purely as an accident.

3. The "Agate" which is a form of ash-grey colour.

All these came from what Gill calls "natural mutation" and limited the colours available to combinations of green, cinnamon and a light colour in various shades.

From 1900 onwards scientific breeding started in earnest. The Agate was produced in Holland (presumably a duplication of the earlier breeding by Hervieux although this is not positive). The breeder was Mr P.J. Helder and it was from this breeding result that there was interest in *colour breeding*.

Various crosses were tried out, such as Greens with Whites, and Cinnamons with Whites, so that Blues and Fawns were produced. In the U.K. Mr L.P. Luke was the first breeder in 1926, but Mrs Martin of New Zealand had bred them 12 years earlier.

Dr Hans Duncker of Germany carried out much of the early work on colour canaries and showed how different colours could be produced. His published work which stimulated interest in colour canaries and to the long period of experimentation to breed the Red Factor canary. The way to success was suggested by Dr Duncker and was finally achieved by A.K. Gill with a cross of a hooded siskin and a canary. He produced a deep orange with a reddish tinge.

ALTERNATIVE VIEWPOINT

At least one authority disagrees with the theory that all canaries originated via Italy as described above. Rudolph Galloway (in *Canaries, Hybrids and British Birds*, S.H. Lewer) asserts that the Elba incident has been used to justify a single source when, in fact, there were many:

1. Canaries in the Canary Islands were probably domesticated long before they were introduced into Europe.

2. The Azores contains many birds including canaries and these were taken to England, Belgium and France at least 30 years before the introduction to other European countries.

3. A natural habitat of the canary is Madeira and birds could have been taken from there to other places.

The argument in favour of assuming a wider and earlier distribution is based on the fact that the islands were owned by different principal countries (France, Spain and Portugal) and ships were calling and taking cargoes aboard (including birds). These exports were going on into Europe quite separate from and, possibly before, the Elba ship wreck.

From 1478 is the date suggested, but there is no positive evidence until around 1660.

This Elba incident took place in 1622. Many writers are of the opinion that canaries were held in captivity before that date and the birds which came from Elba represented only part of the number of canaries being kept. Dr Karl Russ *(Canary Birds: How to Breed for Profit or Pleasure)* states that the Spaniards had a monopoly of trade in canaries for almost a century before the Elba ship wreck. They kept the trade to themselves by selling cock birds only; without the hens no breeding was possible.

DESCRIPTIONS OF THE EARLY CANARIES

According to Barnesby (ibid) the earlier canaries were Lizard, London Fancy and Cinnamon, but he notes that one writer listed 28 varieties as early as 1708! He was refering to Hervieux and his work *Traite des Serims de Canarie.*

The list with additional notes is as follows:

1. *Serin Gris commun.* (The ordinary grey Canary.)
2. *Serin Gris aux duvets** et aux pattes blanches, qu'on appelle Race de Panachez.* (Slightly variegated Frilled Canary with white feet.)
3. *Serin Gris à queue blanche, race de Panachez.* (Slightly variegated Canary with white tail).) -
4. *Serin Blond commun.* (The ordinary Pale Canary.)
5. *Serin Blond aux yeux rouges.* (The Pale Canary with pink eyes.)
6. *Serin Blond doré.* (The Pale canary glossed with yellow.)
7. *Serin Blond aux duvets, race de Panachez.* (Slightly variegated Pale Frilled Canary.)
8. *Serin Bond à queue blanche, race de Panachez.* (Slightly variegated Pale Canary with white tail.)

*"*Duvets*" means the light feathers which adorn the under-surface of the body of birds, and many be translated downy or frilled—for it is this part of the bird that first shows the tendency to excess of feather seen in Dutch Frills. Hervieux's explantion of "*le duvet,*" at page 271, may be translated as follow: "which shows itself, when taking your Canary in your hand, you find on it, on blowing it under the body and stomach, a little white down (*un petit duvet blanc*), and in consequence of a different colour from the natural plumage." He also adds: "There are some Canaries which have much more of this down than others. This is what one finds with the fanciers; one they call *Serins au petit duvet,* that is to say, those which show a little, and the others they call *Serins au grand duvet,* that is to say, those which have much; this down does not appear usually till near the moult."

9. *Serin Jaune commun.* (The lemon-yellow Canary.)
10. *Serin Jaune aux duvets, race de Panachez.* (Slightly variegated Frilled lemon-yellow Canary.)

11. *Serin Jaune à queue blanche, race de Panachez.* (Slightly variegated lemon-yellow Canary, with white tail.)
12. *Serin Agate commun.* (The *original* Lizard Canary.)
13. *Serin Age aux yeux rouges.* (The Lizard with pink eyes, showing cinnamon origin.)
14. *Serin Agate à queue blanche, race de Panachez.* (Slightly variegated Lizard Canary with white tail.)
15. *Serin Agate aux duvets, race de Panachez.* (Slightly variegated Frilled Lizard.)
16. *Serin Isabelle commun.* The *original* cinnamon Canary.)
17. *Serin Isabelle aux yeux rouges.* The cinnamon Canary with pink eyes.)
18. *Serin Isabelle doré.* (The cinnamon Canary glossed with yellow.)
19. *Serin Isabelle aux duvets, race de Panachez.* (Slightly variegated Frilled cinnamon.)
20. *Serin Isabelle à queue blanche, race de Panachez.* (Slightly variegated cinnamon with white tail.)
21. *Serin Blanc, aux yeux rouges.* (The white Canary with pink eyes.)
22. *Serin Panaché commun.* (The *original* variegated Canary.)
23. *Serin Panaché aux yeux rouges.* (Grey-variegated Canary with pink eyes.)
24. *Serin Panaché de blond.* (Pale cinnamon-variegated Canary.)
25. *Serin Panaché de blond aux yeux rouges.* (Pale cinnamon-variegated Canary with pink eyes.)
26. *Serin Panaché de noir.** (Green-variegated Canary.)
27. *Serin Panaché de noir-jonquille aux yeux rouges.* (Cinnamon-green variegated Canary with pink eyes.)
28. *Serin Panaché de noir-jonquille et regulier.* (The London Fancy Canary.)
29. *Serin Plein, qui sont à present les plus rares.* (Clear orange-yellow Canary, which is at present the rarest.)†
(30.‡ The Crest Canary—or rather, the Crowned—which is one of the most beautiful.—Buffon.)

Noir.—Such quills and tail-feathers are mostly black or smoky when spread out, but when in position show their yellowish-green edging mainly.
† Hervieux gives the Paris prices of Canaries in 1713; they gradually increase in price along his list from "Serin Gris commun" at 2l.10s. (two livres ten sous—two shillings and fivepence) to "Serin plein et parfait" at 45l. (£2 5s.)
‡ In the 1793 London edition of "Buffon's Natural History," class 30 is included in Hervieux's 1713 list of varieties, where I have been unable to find it. All the varieties except 29 and 30 are mentioned in the 1709 and 1711 editions of Hervieux.
List from *Canaries, Hybrids and British Birds*, John Robson (c 1920).

GROUP OF PRIZEWINNERS FROM AROUND 1920

3

THE DOMESTICATED CANARY "MAN MADE" VARIETIES

Yorkshire

Border Fancy

Crested

Norwich

Popular Breeds of 50 Years Ago

From the original wild canary, described earlier, a number of different species or "breeds" have developed. These were produced by careful selection and gradually, over many years, specific attributes have been developed.

At times the emphasis has been on song capabilities with the Roller-type canary (the Hartz canary) developed in Germany. Later other "points" were introduced so that distinct varieties began to emerge. Examples are:

(a) **Weight**
(b) **Feathering**
(c) **Size**
(d) **Colour**
(e) **Crest**
(f) **Markings** (eg; Lizard Canary)

Over the years different features have been given prime importance (eg; slimness — Yorkshire Canary) and some characteristics have been lost altogether (eg; the Crest in the Norwich Canary). New breeds such as the Gloster Fancy Canary, Fife Canary and Colour canaries have appeared on the scene. The wee Fife Canary is the latest example of the skills in breeding demonstrated by the enthusiastic fancier.

EVOLUTION OF THE BREEDS

The development of the modern canary is difficult to follow for many reasons:

(a) Records were not always kept.
(b) Descriptions of colours (eg; by Hervieux) do not always agree with modern interpretations.*
(c) Differences of opinion by early writers on the origins of the species or "breeds".
(d) Changes in the *standard* and type; eg; Norwich Canary included the Crested Variety, but is now a Plainhead.
(e) Some breeds are now extinct; eg; London Fancy Canary and Lancashire Coppy (although Lancashire canaries are now being revived by selective breeding).
(f) The evolution of *some* breeds has been quite remarkable in the sense that type has changed drastically, whereas others have not changed at all. Compare the Yorkshire Canary development and the Lizard Canary which has varied very little from its early form.

---

* **See article by Gill referred to in Chapter 2.**

Bearing these factors in mind it is possible to see a definite pattern over a time scale:

1. **1450 onwards** - - The Wild Canary.

2. **1650** — Domestication and the basic mutations by natural selection; White, Cinnamon and Ash-Grey (Agate)

3. **Period 1750 to 1850** — Earlier breeds began to be developed. They are as follows:

   (a) **Lizard Canary** — one of the earliest canaries it was introduced by Huguenot refugees to Britain possibly as early as pre-1750, but no one is sure of the exact date. The standard varieties are *gold* and *silver* but other colours have been produced; eg; Blue, Red, but these are not recognised by the Lizard Canary Association.

   (b) **Norwich Plainhead** — kept in and around the city of Norwich from quite early times, this breed was once the most popular and still remains a great favourite.

   (c) **Roller** — the German song Canary (the Hartz Canary)

   (d) **Old Dutch** — similar in type to the Belgian where it was probably developed.

   (e) **Belgian**   ) Both may have been developed from the

   (f) **Scotch Fancy**   ) "Old Dutch Variety"

   (g) **Frilled** — said to have originated around 1800 and then spread to other countries.

   (h) **Lancashire** — around 1830 and then became extinct, but is now being revived.

   (i) **Crested Norwich** (now extinct) — a very old breed which lost ground to the Plainhead.

4. **Period 1851 to 1950** From the Victorians came new developments and, typically, they excelled in type and colour. They included:

   (a) **Border Fancy** — the "Wee Gem" from the border counties where it is the most popular breed today.

   (b) **Modern Scotch Fancy** — developed from the earlier breed which was judged on the way the bird posed itself (a *bird of position*). Subsequent crosses with the Belgain gave it a longer neck, but some fanciers believe that it also introduced faults.*

   (c) **Yorkshire** — which came into existence around 1890, the first Yorkshire Canary Club being formed in 1897.

---

* See *The Lizard Canary and Other Rare Breeds*, G.T. Dodwell, p 119.

(d) **Crested Canaries** — appear in their modern form in this later period, although Crested birds (including the Crested Norwich) had been around in the eighteenth century. Subsequently new blood was introduced to produce the present-day bird which is classified as a Rare Variety.*

(e) **Gloster Fancy Canary** — was just shown in 1925 and is a diminutive canary produced from the Crested, Roller and Border canaries.

(f) **Colour Canaries** — a breed which was produced from a study of genetics with subsequent application to the breeding of canaries for *colour*. The development took place from 1900 onwards but seriously from the 1920s.

5. **Period 1950 onwards** — Canaries are still very popular and although the rate of development has slowed down, there are still changes taking place. The main new breed is the Fife Fancy Canary which is really a miniature or bantam (introduced in or around 1957).

In addition, Colour Canaries have developed further, including the Red Factor Canary mentioned earlier.

CLASSIFICATIONS

Canaries have been classified in a variety of ways and an understanding of the bases help to appreciate how the breeds developed. Possibilities are as follows:

1. **Territorial or Regional**
2. **Song**
3. **Colour and Markings**
4. **Body characteristics** eg: Crest, feathering or method of standing.

Territorial

The distinct breeds were developed within specific areas or territories and then were taken up nationally and even internationally. The growth of cottage industry in different areas is thought to be one of the main factors.* Thus the breeds originated as:

(a) **Lancashire**	(g) **Gibber Italicus**
(b) **Yorkshire**	(h) **Parisian Frills**
(c) **Norwich**	(i) **Scotch Fancy**
(d) **Border**	(j) **Belgian**
(e) **Gloster**	(k) **Dutch Frill**
(f) **Fife**	(l) **London Fancy**

* See *Canaries*, C.A. House, London, 1923

A White Frilled Canary around 1930. A 1st Prize winner

It will be seen that the locations are by area and by country. Sadly, as interests turned to other pastimes, some of the local breeds such as the Lancashire Coppy and London Fancy have disappeared altogether.

Some believe that the growth of large scale industry contributed to the break-up of the strong local groups of fanciers. Whether this is true or not is difficult to state with exactness, but it does seem clear that interest declined in local areas and as a result the breeds became Yorkshire **types** or Norwich **types** rather than belonging to that particular area.

Song

The original canary was kept for its singing qualities. From early times the song bird has been held in high esteem but, in the Hartz Mountain district of Germany the Song Canary was developed to a high degree of excellence. These birds have now become known as Roller canaries and are distinct from the other breeds.

Song canaries are kept throughout the world, mainly as Hartz or Roller, but there is also an American Song canary of a distinct type.

Colour and Markings

The Colour Canaries, noted earlier, are the best example of classification by colour. In addition, there is the Lizard Canary in its gold or silver version with its scalloped markings which are supposed to resemble the lizard. This is one of the older breeds and as G.T. Dodwell* states: "Its unique feather pattern and changes of plumage make it at once the most beautiful and the most interesting of all breeds, for it is now the only canary that is bred entirely for its markings".

Body Characteristics

There is some overlap with the other types simply because a breed known by a region, eg; Border canary, is also required to stand in a specific manner — pointing semi-erect at an angle of some 60 degrees to the perch.

A more positive indication of birds which are classified by body characteristic can be found in the Scotch Fancy Canary and Belgian Canary as "birds of position". The way they stand is regarded as an *essential* feature of the standard type.

"Crests" are another type of characteristic and the size and quality of the crest on an individual bird is regarded as the most important requirement.

A further feature is the "frill" found on the frilled varieties of canary. The important difference from normal canaries is that the feathers curl and grow outwards into a cape; there is also a frilly front and a thigh frill

---

* *The Lizard Canary and other Rare Breeds*

on each leg. Birds are bred to emphasize the frills on "Mantle", "Jabot" (front), and "Flanks".

In addition to the above, there is also the matter of size. Great importance is attached to this requirement and although not a prime characteristic in itself, no breed can be recognized without reference to size. For example, the Fife Canary must be small or it is not a typical bird of this breed. Accordingly, any tendency for a Fife Canary to look large and clumsy would lead to disqualification.

4

BRIEF OUTLINE OF THE

POPULAR VARIETIES

The Belgian Canary

INTRODUCTION

As in all things fashions come and go, changes are made, certain fads or fancies are adopted, and the whole process goes through a cycle which is constantly changing. The canary Fancy is no exception and a breed that was very popular falls out of favour and is replaced by others. Indeed, some breeds such as the London Fancy Canary have disappeared altogether whereas others such as the Lancashire are being·revived.

At one time the Norwich canary was the best known and is still very popular but now the Border reigns supreme and others challenge for places in the popularity stakes. Even now breeds such as the Fife appear on the scene and struggle in obscurity until they become popular.

What follows are brief descriptions of the canary breeds still to be seen. Where there is very little literature available a more extensive coverage has been given. The reader is advised to consult the list of titles of books available and refer to the one most appropriate to his breed:

1. **Belgian Canary** (now very scarce)
2. **Border Fancy Canary** (at present the most popular breed)
3. **Coloured Canaries** (colours follow a complex classification; recommended for those fanciers who like a challenge)
4. **Crested Canaries** (another rare breed)
5. **Fife Fancy Canary** (the bantam of the Canary Fancy)
6. **Frilled Canaries** (five breeds included in this group)
7. **Gloster Fancy Canary** (now well established as a small crest breed)
8. **Lancashire Canary** (scarce but being revived — a Giant Canary)
9. **Lizard Canary** (very old variety bred for patterns and markings of plumage)
10. **Norwich Canary** (one of the top canaries)
11. **Red Canary** (included under Colour Canaries)
12. **Roller Canary** (the song bird of the Canary World)
13. **Scotch Fancy** (a rare breed of unusual stature)
14. **Yorkshire Canary** (a very popular breed)

THE BELGIAN CANARY

This is a very scarce breed which has had an unsettled history. In the early days of showing it played a major role and later it was used for developing other show canaries.

Today the Belgian canary is seldom seen. It is the "hunch-back" of the Fancy this being a prominent feature. With its small head, long neck and elongated body, resting on stilt-like legs, this bird is a wonder to behold.

When judged it should be viewed from the point of view of the following:

1. **Position** — the way it stands with a stance of 90° posture is given 40 points in the *standard* from a total of 100.
2. **Type** — the sum total of the major features which make up the specific breed.

The show cage is the open wire type and is illustrated in the Chapter which deals with shows.

The origin of the Belgian is doubtful; but while it may be thought that the low carriage of the head is due to standing on a perch placed so near the top of the cage that the poor creature could not lift its head up without hurting itself, it must have had room enough to dispose of its tail, for that forms a perfectly perpendicular line with the back. Some of these birds have a more or less developed frill on the breast, indicating a connection with the Dutch type of Canary, which is described as *frisé et jaboté* — that is to say, curled and frilled; and some of them are curiously marked and mottled. One that is much admired is buff in body-colour, with a cap and saddle of a very dark slate-colour, which give it the appearance of wearing a short mantle; this, however, must not touch the wings, but be confined to the back proper.

Belgian Canaries as a rule are very good parents when properly lodged and treated; but they are also as a rule very nervous and timid, and resent being interfered with. While it is advised to meddle as little as possible with any breeding Canary, the caution is particularly necessary in the case of the Belgian, and one authority was so impressed with its importance, that he said, under no circumstances should a Belgian Canary be handled.

On account of the bird's configuration and the depressed position of the head, it is a good plan to place a perch about 1½in. or 2in. above the nest, and at one side of it, on which the parents can take their stand when feeding the little ones. When so accommodated, they appear to be more at their ease than if compelled to stand on the edge of the nest itself when occupied by satisfying the wants of their offspring.

A good many nostrums, some of the most unlikely kind, have been recommended for the use of Belgian Canaries engaged in rearing their young; but the simpler the diet the more likely is success to be attained. Accustomed as the birds have been for many generations to a stimulating diet of egg, they do not seem to get on very well without it, and the "no-egg system" is not recommended for them — at least, if they are valuable birds, and their owner has no mind to make them the subject of experiments.

The Belgian, perhaps, is not a great favourite in this country certainly not a general one; but it has its admirers nevertheless, and we can certainly make room for it.

THE BORDER FANCY CANARY

For a full and detailed account of this breed the reader is referred to *The Border Canary* by Joe Bracegirdle. Without doubt it is now the most popular breed and the fact that specimens are readily available at realistic prices helps the growth of its popularity.

The breed has no special features such as a crest or long legs, but it is a beautifully symmetrical bird, with ideal proportions. Plumage should be close and of a fine quality. Birds with coarse features should not be tolerated.

Over the years the Border has become a stouter bird, although it is still nothing near the size of the Norwich. These birds used to be called "wee gems", but development of the body has made this description a misnomer.

Colour feeding is prohibited, so on no account should it be practised.

COLOURED CANARIES

These used to be termed the *New* Coloured Canaries, but the "new" has been omitted. Heading the list is the *Red Canary* and there are other colours which have been developed as imitations. The ideal length is 5 inches.

A wide variety of colours is possible and some have quite long and complex descriptions; eg; Frosted Gold Isabel Pastel. The terms used to show the Background colour are:

1. **Agate** to describe the Green in dilute form.
2. **Isabel** which is a dilute Cinnamon.

We finish up with descriptions such as "Gold Isabel Pastel" which means a gold bird with a cinnamon background. Rules are laid down to describe the colours which should be evenly distributed.

Readers interested are advised to refer to a specialist book on Colour Canaries.

CRESTED CANARIES

The Crested Canary is a very old breed which has undergone a number of changes. In Victorian times it had a very strong following, but was developed into a Norwich **Crested** which fell out of favour and

The Border Convention
Model Bird

The Border Canary —
now the most popular '

A Typical Coloured
Canary Showing the Type

subsequently was dropped altogether. The Norwich then continued as a Norwich **Plainhead** instead of the two types side by side.

Obviously, as the name implies, the bird should have a large crest which has a small centre. In size it is similar to the Norwich Canary from which many people believe it came. Accordingly, around 6½ inches is the recommended length. It differs from the Gloster which is a *diminutive* bird of not more than 4¾ inches and the Lancashire Canary (Lancashire Coppy) which is a giant of a bird of 7 to 8 inches, which has a large droopy crest.

THE FIFE CANARY

Many fanciers regard the Fife Fancy Canary as a miniature of the Border Canary. Indeed, except for its size, which must not exceed 4¼ inches, the two breeds are extremely similar.

The fact remains that the Fife must be small and the diminutive size allows a much shorter back and a more compact body. The nicely rounded chest should be surmounted by a small head which is round and neat, with beak to match and eyes centred.

The normal colours such as green, yellow, Buff are allowed but these should be rich, soft and pure with no harshness or exaggeration such as that given from colour feeding. The Fife should be a lively character, full of vitality.

FRILLED BREEDS

The frilled breeds are so named because of the curled feathers which appear on the body of the canary. Each type has its own characteristics; thus:

1. **North Dutch Frill** — Frills appear on the *breast*, the back (the "mantle") and the *flanks*. Stance 85°.
2. **South Dutch Frill** — In effect this is the Belgian Canary with frills. Accordingly, it has the hump-backed appearance of the Belgian, but with frills similar to the North Dutch Frill. However, this is a generalisation and the reader should consult a book on the breed for full details (eg; *Canary Standards in Colour*, G.T. Dodwell)
3. **Gibber Italicus** — The Gibber Italicus is similar to the South Dutch Frill, but of smaller stature. It is, like the S.D.F., a bird of posture and achievement of the figure "7" is of great importance. The frilling is not as pronounced. Size is around 14cm. and the stance is 90° making it a very upright bird.
4. **The Padovan Frill** — The Padovan Frill Canary possesses **frills and a crest** as well. It is a large bird with an upright position (65°

Yellow Variegated Dutch Crest (around 1900)

Fife Canary — the bantam of canaries

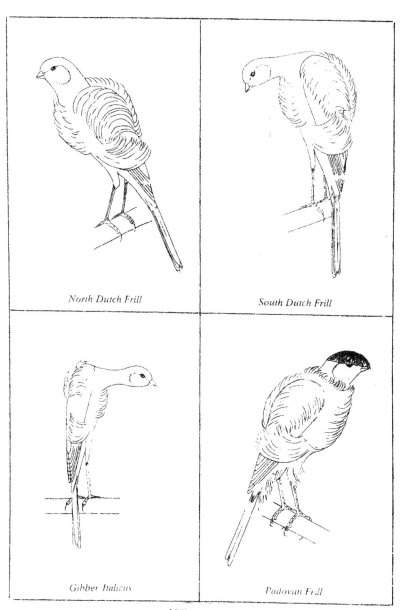

North Dutch Frill

South Dutch Frill

Gibber Italicus

Padovan Frill

FRILLED BREEDS

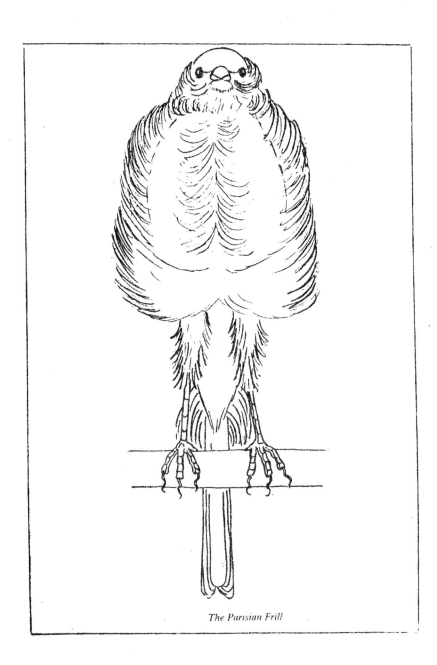

The Parisian Frill

stance), but not as upright as the birds described earlier in this section. As regards the plumage this should follow the lines of the North Dutch Canary.

5. **The Parisian Frill** — This canary is the giant of the Frills having a size of around 21cm. (around 8½ inches). The frills are also copious, there being distinct sections which cover the entire body. The frills come up to the head and form a collar rather like a Hun pigeon. There is also a sub-variety the **Milan Frill**.

This most extraordinary bird is the more popular of the Frilled canaries but even so is still regarded as a rare variety.

GLOSTER CANARY

The Gloster Canary is an example of breeding that was regarded as impossible — a small crested bird when previously all canaries with crests had been gigantic birds. Yet it was achieved in 1925 and today it graces the show benches as being one of the most attractive and graceful of all the breeds.

There are two types of Gloster:

1. **The Corona** or Crested.
2. **The Consort** or Plainhead.

Both possess the same body type and may be male or female in either description. Their plumage is close and fine with the crest or corona small with a neat centre.

The body shape follows the *orthodox shape* of such birds as the Border or Norwich although obviously there are differences in terms of bulkiness and the Border is much more upright.

THE LANCASHIRE CANARY

Perhaps the grandest variety of all — certainly the biggest — is the Lancashire Canary. It may be crested (the Coppy) or Plainhead.

Perhaps, if I may be allowed to express an opinion, the plainheaded Lancashire is the finer bird of the two: at least, it has the entire use of its full, beady, black eyes; while its relative with the crest can only look in a downward direction to its feet, and this restricted vision gives the bird an air of timidity and restlessness that detracts from its merits in some eyes.

As in every other variety of the Canary, we find rich yellow Lancashire Coppies and Plainheads, others that are buff, and yet others that are mottled; but the big green birds one occasionally meets with belong rather to the Dutch race than the British, and are not much

Corona

Consort

Gloster Canaries

admired in this country. The chief characteristic of the last-named is a ruff, or frill, of exceedingly long feathers on the breast, where they are sometimes curled in a remarkable manner resembling the shirt-frills of the dandies in the days of the Regency and when George the Fourth was king.

The biggest plainhead I have handled measured 7¾in. from the point of the bill to the extremity of the tail, and was a noble-looking creature. I doubt if this dimension has been exceeded, but that is no reason why still finer birds should not be bred, if fanciers will only set their minds upon getting them, and break the record that obtains at present.

The points of a plainhead Lancashire Canary are: First, size, that is length and bulk. The head must be broad, not too round, and the eyes must be surmounted with eyebrows, heavy, but not interfering with the vision. The breast feathers, not too long, must have no tendency to curl or form a frill. The general condition must be sound and vigorous, so that the bird can hop about freely, and show no symptom of lethargy or dullness. The wings must be held tightly against the body, and the tail should be straight — that is, should form a continuous line with the back, and not dip below or stand out above it. Every shade of colour has its special admirers, and no hard and fast line can be laid down in regard to a favourite tint, but whether jonque, buff, or evenly or unevenly ticked, the colour should be uniform, and not graduated one way or another.

The Coppy proper differs from the Lancashire Plainhead in possessing a crest, and is sometimes called a "turn-crown". Its points are identical with those of the Plainhead, and in addition it is judged by the crest, the individual feathers of which are oval in shape, and regularly and evenly disposed; they may be of the same colour as the rest of the plumage, or darker, but are scarcely ever of a lighter shade, and the dark crest is thought to be more effective than the light one, affording, as it does, a marked contrast to the rest of the body.

The one drawback, as already observed, to the crest is that it overlaps the eyes, and prevents the bird from seeing anything above or beside it, its range of vision only extending in a downward direction. However, in a cage that is of comparatively slight consequence, and as these valuable birds are seldom, if ever, committed to the risks and dangers inseparable from a life of comparative freedom in an aviary, the point is not of so much importance as if the crested birds were in full enjoyment of their liberty.

Everything intended for the use and convenience of these giants of Canarydom, whether crested or plainheaded, must be on a larger scale than for their lesser brethren — more extensive cages, roomier nests, bigger receptacles for seed and water, and thicker perches, which, however, should not be all of the same size, but of different thicknesses,

Crested or Coppy

Plainhead

Lancashire Canaries (Reduced in Size)

like the branches of a tree, so that the feet may be rested, and not cramped by always grasping a perch of the same size.

These great birds are not always as good parents as they might be, and where a pair are known to have neglected their duty, or to have performed it only in a perfunctory manner, it will be better to distribute their valuable eggs among some common birds of reliable character — one or two eggs to each — so that the foster-parents' care and attention may be concentrated on a single nestling, or, at most, on two young ones, which would thus have a greater chance of developing into fine specimens of their race.

It is astonishing how large even a common Canary will become if it is the only child of its parents or foster-parents, compared with others that are hatched and brought up in the ordinary way, four or five together in a nest. Consequently, if it is desired to have big birds, one egg only should be allowed to hatch. The attention of the old birds being concentrated upon it, the young bird will develop to its utmost capacity, and if this course is adopted with its progeny, and so on, there is scarcely any limit to the dimensions that may in time be reached. But of course good food, as well as good feeding, is indispensable.

I do not recommend colour-feeding for the Lancashire Canary which looks best, I think, in its natural plumage. Should others be of a different opinion, it will be better to reserve the process until the young bird's first moult, and not to give the colouring food while it is in the nest, so as to avoid the possibility of its interfering with the youngster's growth.

It is not advisable to permit the hen to lay too many eggs in the season, so that it will be necessary to substitute one or two eggs of a common bird for her own, and allow her to sit upon them and bring up the nestlings, or at least make an attempt to do so.

Sadly these birds are now very scarce, but a revival is being attempted.

THE LIZARD CANARY

This is the most distinct variety that has yet been produced in the Canary world. The name of "Lizard" has been bestowed upon this Canary owing to the fancied resemblance of the scalloped markings on its back and sides to the scales of its reptilian namesake. It can scarcely be termed a happy or an appropriate one: however, it is consecrated by long usage, and is likely to remain. Its origin is quite unknown, though a number of conjectures have been hazarded as to its parentage, one of the most unlikely being that it is a cross between the ordinary Canary and the Saffron Sparrow (misnamed Finch). The latter is a Brazilian species, with which the Canary has nothing in common beyond the fact that they are both small birds, for one builds an open nest, and the other rears its brood in a hole in a tree, rock, or building. The cock Canary feeds its mate and young with food disgorged from its crop, and the male Saffron Sparrow carries food to its offspring in its bill, as the Sparrows and Buntings do, and does not feed its mate. The eggs of the two species are also quite unlike: those of the Canary, as everybody knows, are blue, pale blue, or bluish-green, spotted and speckled with reddish-brown; while those of the Saffron Sparrow very much resemble those of the common House Sparrow.

Two Types

There are two principal types of the Lizard Fancy, namely, the **golden-spangled** and the **silver-spangled**, the former being perhaps the more beautiful of the two. In a well-bred bird of either sub-division the top of the head is covered with a cap, which should be of primrose (or, rather, crocus yellow), unmixed with a single feather of any other shade — the cap is said to be "broken" if any such intrude upon it. Deep-coloured in the golden-spangled, the cap is much paler in the silver-spangled Lizard, and the lighter markings on the back and sides correspond in colour with that of the cap and the under-parts of the body.

It is a pity to mar the extreme delicacy of the natural colours of these birds by giving them colour-food (although allowed), which has the effect of confusing the two races, for by its action a pale cap becomes golden, and a bright yellow is turned into red.

The Lizard Canary is one of the smaller varieties, rarely exceeding 6in. in length, and sometimes not attaining even that. So much care has been expended on the development of the "spangle", golden or silver, that the cap has been neglected, and is rather rarely met with in a perfect state. So well, indeed, is this recognised that classes for "broken caps" have been instituted at the principal Canary shows, which seems to be equivalent to offering a premium for spoiling one of the most attractive features of this favourite variety. The spangle is important, no doubt, and the body-colour no less so, but the cap ought not to be neglected either, and breeders will be well advised to cultivate it more than has appeared to be the case lately.

The greatest drawback in breeding Lizard Canaries is that the perfection of the plumage only lasts for one year. In their nest-feathers the young birds are not spangled at all, and but for the characteristic cap (yellow or buff, as the case may be) could not be distinguished from ordinary green canaries. But with the second change of feathers the spangles make their appearance in all their glory, to deteriorate at every successive moult until the birds once more, in their maturity and age, revert to their original appearance. The Lizard is rather loose-feathered, too, and should on no account be handled, or it will be very apt to lose an essential part of its plumage from wings or tail or shoulders, which would be fatal to all hope of success on the show bench.

Some judges attach most importance to the cap, others to the distinctive spangle, and it is rare to find a bird possessing both distinctions in perfection; still, it is a standard that might be bred up to, and would not be more difficult to attain than it is to get other points not only in the various breeds of poultry and pigeons, but also in the case of the birds under consideration.

A word or two with reference to the mating of Lizard Canaries will bring us to the conclusion of this part of the subject. Many fanciers do not begin to breed from them till they are three years old. In the first year, it is said, the birds are immature, and their offspring lack the distinctive characters that mark the adult or perfect Lizard; and in the second they are in their prime, and too valuable on the show bench to admit of their time being wasted on a task that can be better accomplished later on.

When breeding it is usual to pair a yellow-capped cock with a silver or mealy hen; but some breeders think this is a mistake, on the grounds that "Like produces like". Therefore it is argued if golds are wanted, golds must be mated with each other; and to obtain buffs or silvers, these should be paired together: the result in both cases will be satisfactory.

Although necessarily more or less inbred, probably from their first appearance, the Lizard so far has shown little or no sign of deterioration either in appearance or in stamina. As a rule, it is a hardy bird, and with ordinary care will live as long in a cage as any ordinary canary.

For many reasons, it is better to keep and breed the Lizards in roomy cages than to turn them adrift in bird-room or aviary, in which, mating as they listed, they would quickly deteriorate in one essential point or another.

THE NORWICH CANARY

The Norwich is altogether a shorter and stouter bird than the Yorkshire, for its girth is half as much again as that of the latter, and its length runs from 6in. to 6¼in.

If the two varieties already dealt with offer several well-established variations, the Norwich is more erratic in that respect than either of them. It is also more prone to put on colour than they are. As a rule, Norwich Canaries are good parents, and rarely require assistance to rear their young.

As in the case of the other varieties, we have yellow Norwich

Cock

Hen

Lizard Canaries

Canaries, buffs, regularly marked or ticked, and other that are blotched and self-coloured. The yellow birds assume a deep orange-red colour when moulted on colour food.

G.T. Dodwell, *Canary Standards in Colour*, describes the Norwich as follows:

> The modern type of Norwich should, above all, possess a good head, large and well rounded with great width across the skull in both directions. Ideally, there should be no suggestion of any overhanging eyebrows and the eye itself should be clear and bright. The beak should be short and stout and the cheeks well filled to give the bird a chubby appearance. Any bird with poor head qualities, whatever its other merits, would have little chance of success on the show bench.
>
> The neck should be short and thick connecting the broad, round head almost imperceptibly with the equally broad and well rounded body. This body may be described as exactly the opposite of those breeds that possess a long and finely drawn outline, as it is both short and compact and with great depth through from the back to the breast. The back should be short, broad and almost straight, showing but a very slight rise transversely. The chest is both deep and wide and should be well rounded in one continuous curve from throat to tail.
>
> The wings and tail, following the trend of all the other features, should also be short and compact. As with most breeds of canary the wings must be tightly braced and held close to the body, with the tips of the flight feathers in line, and ending just above the root of the tail. This, too, should be closely folded, or "piped", and must be held in continuation of the line of the body, being neither drooping nor held high in the "robin-tailed" position.
>
> The legs and feet should be strong and well formed and well set back to carry the bird in the normal position of about 45 degrees from the horizontal. Unlike some other breeds, the Norwich is not a bird of positon as such but should carry itself well and move quite briskly and not in a slovenly manner.

THE ROLLER CANARY*

The Roller Canary, known as the Hartz or simply German Canary is, as a rule, the smallest of its race, many specimens measuring no more than 5in. or 5¼in. in total length. Most of them are buff in colour — buff of the faintest shade, verging on white — but a few show a trace of yellow, and others are piebald or mottled.

If insignificant in point of size and depth of colouring, compared with the larger and more brilliantly coloured breeds already considered, the Roller Canary excels them all as a vocalist, and it is nothing short of marvellous how one small throat can pour forth the volume of sweet sounds one may hear proceeding from a well-trained Roller; no less than twenty-seven distinct changes have been counted in the song of one of these remarkable birds.

* See: *The Roller Canary* Revised by George Preskey

Figure 4-11 A Typical Norwich Canary

Figure 4-12 A Roller Canary — the Song Bird of the Canary World

Of course this proficiency is not attained without painstaking teaching, continued through many generations, and a good performer is worth a lot of money.

The food of the Roller Canary too, differs from that upon which our English and Scotch birds are usually nourished, and consists for the most part of egg food, soaked rape-seed and spray-millet. A sudden change to hard and dry canary-seed, to which our birds are accustomed, not infrequently upsets the little Roller, gives him indigestion and all its concomitant evils, shortening his life, and spoiling, when it does not altogether silence, his great charm — his song.

THE SCOTCH FANCY CANARY

If the Yorkshire, and more especially the Norwich, are the favourites with most fanciers south of the Tweed, amateurs residing north of that historic stream have a type of their own, which is known as the Scotch Fancy or Glasgow Don, and is rather peculiar-looking. In configuration it bears considerable resemblance to the Yorkshire, and no doubt owes its origin to that elegantly-shaped and beautifully-coloured bird; indeed, older fanciers believed that it may have arisen in the first instance from one of the latter canaries having been kept in a cage that was not high enough to permit of his standing in his usually characteristic upright attitude. The cage in which he was confined being a shallow one, the bird, to prevent himself from knocking his head against the top, would naturally thrust it forward a little; and as there would also be no room for his tail in its normal position, that too was thrust forward under the perch, with the result that his back became rounded, and with the head and tail combined to form the segment of a circle round the perch on which he had to stand in his uncomfortable prison-house. At last, use being second nature, this position became fixed, and was transmitted to his progeny; and selection and judicious management on the part of the breeder gradually produced the type of bird that is now prime favourite in Scotland, and has many admirers in this country too. The origin of the variety has also been attributed to a cross of the Yorkshire with the Belgian, or so-called Belgian, variety; and the Scotch Fancy bird has a prominent shoulder, which give some countenance to the belief, though it does not stick out to the same extent, and the head is never sunk down between the legs, or near them, in the former breed.

The Scotch Fancy Canary is met with in all colours common to its race — yellow, buff, green, and a combination of all three types — but self-coloured birds seem to be more in favour than those that are mottled, ticked, or piebald, the last-named term corresponding to our "heavily variegated", but not so much importance is attached to regularity in the markings as obtains south of the Cheviots.

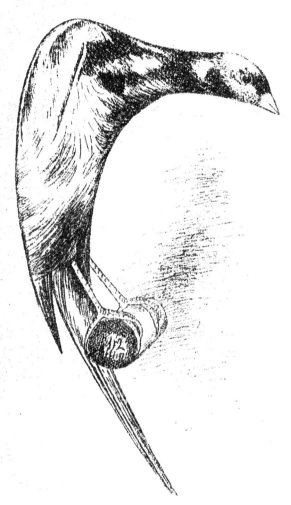

The Scotch Fancy Canary

The Yorkshire Canary
Not as Slim as it Used to Be.

The Scotch Fancy, as a rule, is timid, and not a reliable parent. The young are fed assiduously enough for a few days, and then, the novelty having worn off, are apt to be neglected; so it is as well to be provided with good foster-parents, to whom the eggs of the more valuable birds may be committed, as well as the task of bringing up the young, which are not influenced by their surroundings, and do not renounce the singular position maintained by the parents in favour of the more natural carriage of their nurse.

THE YORKSHIRE CANARY

The Yorkshire Canary is a long, slim bird with an erect carriage. It is a very handsome creature, even if not as imposing in appearance as some breeds.

Self-coloured and evenly-ticked specimens are those that are most in request, and fetch the best price, whilst such as are irregularly marked and blotched are justly held to be inferior.

A fair-sized Yorkshire will measure from 6½in. to 7in. in length, and be scarcely half the girth of the Lancashire Canary. Its position when in repose is very upright, and when in motion much more so, so that a line drawn from the back of the head to the end of the tail will be almost perpendicular.

The cock Yorkshire is usually a good singer, but his voice is sometimes shrill and loud, which is rather the fault of his education than attributable to his idiosyncrasy. Very frequently he repeats the notes of the Skylark, which are too loud for the house, and in point of resonance and force lose nothing by his rendering of them. When the Woodlark has been his tutor, the Yorkshire Canary is a much more pleasing inmate of the drawing-room, where his shriller-voiced brother is altogether out of place.

In selecting birds of this variety for breeding, attention should be paid to the following points: length, slimness of figure, good upright carriage, and a pleasing disposition of colour if the bird is ticked or mottled, or perfect uniformity of tinting if self-coloured, whether yellow, buff, or green.

Roller Canary Singing or Training Cage

Figure 5-1 Domestic Fancy Cage for use in the home

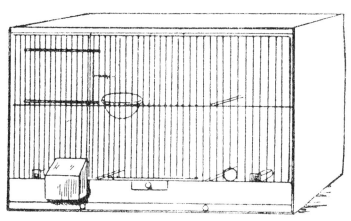

Figure 5-2 Simple Breeding Cage Size: 18" (45.7cm) long x 16" high x 12" deep.
Dimensions depend on breed

Housing birds in *appropriate* cages or aviaries is of vital importance to their health and well-being. If breeding is to be attempted conditions must be excellent or efforts will be wasted.

The fancier's choice will be influenced by what he can afford. Some modern breeders are prepared to sacrifice a great deal to build a purpose-made aviary of brick with windows and ventilation. In the long run such expenditure may well be justified, but many fanciers manage very well with home made sheds and flights.

Cages may serve many purposes — housing, breeding, showing or training. They may be kept in a room in a dwelling house for the pet bird or in a bird room specially made for the purpose. The use of small open cages has long been the subject of criticism. Claude St. John (*Our Canaries*) came to the conclusion that open wire cages should be used only in rooms where there are no variations in temperature and no draughts.

There is now legal recognition that birds should not be kept in small show-type cages for long periods. They are too restricting and, therefore, not recommended for permanent homes.

CAGES

The types of cages found in use are as follows:

1. **Domestic fancy cages** for use in the home.
   These are usually pleasing in design and hang on stands or rest on a small table. For the enthusiast with money to spend on antiques there are some splendid cages which will do justice to the most discerning householder. However, they can be very generous in space with many compartments.

2. **Breeding cages** which may have one or more compartments — single, double or treble. Basically they are wooden boxes with wire fronts. They enable the birds to have privacy.

3. **Nursery cages** for rearing youngsters when feather pecking and bullying takes place.

4. **Show cages** which may be the **open wire type** or **box cages.** The specialist clubs lay down the precise cage to be used for each breed and these must be used in accordance with the regulations of the particular club, the statutory requirements are laid down by the various acts in existence in the UK and in other countries.

AVIARIES

The design of the aviary is of great importance and therefore time should be taken to make sure the best structure possible is made or obtained. This can be attractive as well as functional and, in a garden, landscaping is very appropriate. Lawns, bushes, rustic fences, trellis work and other gardening features all help to create the correct environment.

FUNCTIONAL REQUIREMENTS

Factors to consider when designing an aviary are as follows:

1. Size of house or sleeping shed.
2. Flights including covered section.
3. Insulation and ventilation.
4. Lighting.
5. Protection from disease and predators.
6. Perches and related equipment.
7. Safety porches.
8. Landscaping and Aesthetic Requirements.

The functional requirements cover the essentials for sound management and good health. These can be achieved in a solid building built of corrugated tin, but the impression can be one of make-shift economy which is possibly fine for a smallholding but not for beautiful birds in a garden.

Both wooden and metal structures may be purchased which are pleasing in design. They can be adapted with internal partitions as well as being insulated.

Larger buildings are available in the form of stables or dog kennels and, again, these may be adapted for breeding rooms or indoor aviaries. They are usually of very solid construction and whilst costly they lend themselves to modification without difficulty. They are likely to suit the breeder who wishes to keep and breed a considerable number of birds.

SIZE OF AVIARIES

There is no hard and fast rule on the optimum size aviary. Usually though a minimum size of floor space of 1 square foot (30cm) per bird is taken as a guide, but to allow for breeding around 1 square metre per bird is desirable. At the end of each season the space should be reviewed for young birds hatched can soon cause overcrowding.

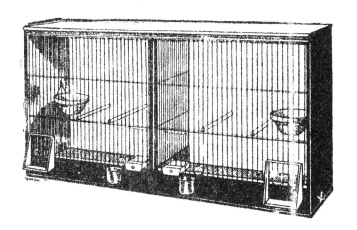

Two-compartment Breeding Cage Size: double single cage In effect 2 cages side by side. Other sizes exist

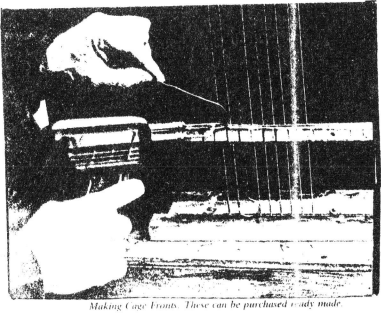

Making Cage Fronts. These can be purchased ready made.

Typical Bird Room

A view often expressed is that *cubic* capacity should not be taken as a guide to the size of aviary required. Whilst this may be the case it is also true that the extent of the flights attached to aviaries will be important in determining whether birds have adequate room. If they are flying around or perching on the flights they will be relieving pressure on the aviary proper (the sleeping apartment).

CONSTRUCTION

Today there are many excellent sheds available from the local garden and bird centres. There are also many very poor structures. Very thin board affixed with wire staples will not last; nor will it give adequate protection to the birds. Avoid such sheds because in the long run the apparent cheapness will prove to be very expensive.

Essentials are as follows:

1. Solid timber preferably lined with some form of insulating board (not soft material which the birds can peck away). Tongue and grooved boarding is very desirable because this avoids draughts. Usually ¾" board (around 30mm) is recommended.

2. The roof should be watertight and easily maintained (a coat of tar and creosote each year should keep it in good order). Perspex sheets give adequate light, but tend to be cold in winter and hot in summer, although they are acceptable for the covered flight which has wire netting on the outside. Boards and roofing felt are probably the best method for keeping the shed dry, but remember that adequate lighting is still essential within the shed.

3. Windows and entrance holes should be provided for adequate light and exits (which also give some ventilation).
Windows should be made so they can be opened, but without draughts and properly wired so that the birds cannot escape through openings. In addition, shutters or circular outlets fitted to the sides may be used for:

   (a) ventilation;
   or
   (b) allowing birds to fly through the openings into the outdoor flights (it may be desirable to close these in winter).

4. The floor should be made of wood (above the ground) or concrete. Thick timber, well supported is esential or rats, mice and other vermin will find their way in. Moreover, if not raised

Aviary Flight and Sleeping Quarters

This Aviary has a large wire flight and commodious sleeping quarters, which are divided by panels, having two windows which can be opened or closed as desired.

The sleeping quarters and flight are entered by separate doors from the safety entrance porch, as shown in the illustration.

An Unusual Aviary. Centre 4' x 3' x 5' high, flights 4' x 2' x 3' high
Note the landscaping to fit in with the surrounds.

above the earth the wood will rot and after a few years will let in damp and cold.

Concrete is obviously the answer, but this tends to be cold so a good covering of clean sawdust is essential (renewed when it becomes soiled). Alternatively, a shed with a wooden floor can be placed on concrete or flagstones.

THE BIRD ROOM

Aviary and **bird-room** tend to be descriptions of the same thing. However, some people prefer to refer to a bird-room as a specially fitted building, or room within a building, where all essentials can be kept and the birds can be housed in considerable comfort. Certainly for successful all-the-year-round management well-built insulated accommodation is vital.

An aviary purchased from a garden centre will probably have all the essentials for keeping a few birds, but it will not provide them with all their needs for successful breeding and showing.

If space permits an aviary and bird-room may be advisable, thus allowing birds to be kept in comfort at all times as well as providing the means of training for shows. Taken to the ultimate there should also be provision for running water indoors and electricity for light and heat.

INSULATION AND VENTILATION

The aviary or bird-room should be insulated so as to avoid extremes in temperature. If a brick building is used then a wooden frame can be built into the structure with some form of cavity and the inner skin would be plaster board, hard board or one of the many special boards now available. Polystyrene tiles are not suitable because they tend to flake and are a fire hazard. However, some manufacturers have produced special insulating materials for commercial poultry sheds and these could well be worth investigating.

VENTILATION

The provision of adequate air without excessive draughts should receive attention. This question is also linked with the provision of windows, which may be allowed to open with metal gauze or wire netting to cover the opening. Small holes drilled in the side of the shed will also provide ventilation as will some form of grill arrangement which will open and close.

Ideally the inlet for air should be towards the top of the building. When the air enters it sinks to the ground and, when warmed up, will rise and may be let out at roof level. If the inlet opening is too near the bottom of the building the inrush of air will be too fierce and will cause discomfort.

The aim should be to get the air to circulate so as to remove any foul air or gases, but not to make the aviary too cold. Accordingly, the outside temperature should be considered and in the summer months wire netting covered openings could be beneficial. In winter a different story emerges because the conservation of heat is important, even if there is some loss of ventilation in the bird-room proper (ie., sleeping quarters). Except on very bad days (cold or wet) the birds should always be allowed access to a flight and thereby breathe a plentiful supply of fresh air.

Some breeders never use any heat in a bird-room, whereas others insist that no results are possible without the means of keeping the temperature at not less than around 50° F.   Certainly for making an early start with breeding and to make sure that water does not freeze some form of heating is advisable.

In modern times the tendency is to employ tubular heaters which are totally enclosed and use a small amount of electricity. A typical heater is shown opposite; it is usually supplied in convenient lengths of around 1 metre and can be fitted easily and requires no maintenance. Because of its low power consumption it may be operated without a thermostat simply being turned off when the weather is mild.

The position of the aviary also affects heat and light. The author has an aviary at the side of a large lawn with hedges on one side and a wire netting front at the other. Any day when there is sun its rays catch the front of the aviary and give light and warmth. On the other hand, a shed and aviary in a wooded area tends to be extremely suitable in the Summer, but is bitterly cold in Winter. In such circumstances the author has had bantams succumb to the severe frosts which accumulate in the trees so imagine what can happen to a minute bird like a canary.

This is not to suggest that small birds such as canaries are not hardy. They will stand considerable cold and variations in weather once acclimatised, but if early breeding is required with fertile eggs from the first clutch of eggs then give them shelter from cold winds, snow and rain.

LIGHTING

Light affects birds and provides the stimulation to lay. Accordingly the provision of adequate light is essential in two forms:

(a) Windows and netted fronts.
(b) Electric light controlled by a time switch so that the desired amount of light can be given.

The cage should be adequately ventilated but draught free. There is no doubt that such a cage is a very useful aid in the treatment of sick birds and I would go so far as to say that no bird room is fully equipped without one. It is true that in a well run bird room the use of a hospital cage is a very infrequent occurence, but if they are needed then they are well worth the effort of making them.

In the absence of a hospital cage, heat can be administered by placing the sick bird in a show cage and covering the top, back and sides with a towel leaving the open front facing the source of heat. The method is not so precise as the use of a hospital cage, however because an even temperature is very difficult to maintain.

Any bird which has been so treated, either in a hospital cage, or as described above should be returned to its normal environment gradually over a period of perhaps two days. Violent fluctuations in temperature can in themselves be the cause of colds and chills and should be avoided.

GENERAL RULES

When a bird is ill, it is important to cause as little disturbance as possible. Avoid all unnecessary movement and keep it in a quiet place away from children, household pets, the television set or any other outside influence which may cause it to be disturbed and perhaps even frightened.

Never attempt to hurry the healing process by giving larger amounts of any given drug than those recommended, which will do more harm than good. Remember that all diseases and illnesses take time to cure and the bird will need time to recover its normal state of health after it has been returned to the bird room.

ONLY SHOW FIT BIRDS

Do not take a bird which has been ill and put it into a show cage and then expect the bird to do well on the show bench, the results of such an action would in all probability be the death of the bird.

If any given treatment is working well, then do not change it in an attempt to heal the bird more quickly. There is a very tried and true maxim in medicine which states that one should never change a treatment which is having the effect for which it is intended.

HYGIENE

There are other diseases and illnesses which can be contracted by canaries, but if the bird room is kept dry, clean and draught proof then there should be very little trouble in this respect. Be very strict as regards disease prevention.

Rules to follow are:

1. Observe birds every day and watch for tell-tale signs.
2. DO NOT TOLERATE DIRT AND DUST.
3. Make sure food and water is always available.
4. Isolate sick birds.
5. Cull birds which are permanently sick or possess serious defects.

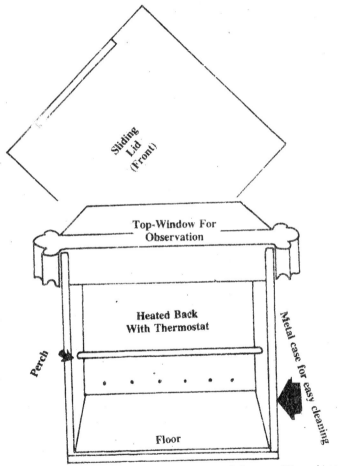

A modern Hospital Cage (courtesy: Bartholomews of Hampshire)

13

BACKGROUND
AND
HISTORY OF
GLOSTER CANARY

An early example of a Yellow Glosier from a painting by H. Norman. Note the long body and poor crest.

TYPE

The Gloster canary is an extremely small bird — usually described as *diminutive* which, according to the *standard,* means not longer than 4.5 inches (11.4 cm).

Other varieties may be used to compare relative sizes:

Border: not to exceed 5.5 inches (14cm)
Norwich: Ideal 6.1 inches (15.5cm)
Lizard: Ideal 4.5 inches (11.4cm)
Yorkshire: Ideal 6.75 inches (17.24cm)
Fife: Ideal 4.25 inches (10.5cm)
Gloster: Ideal 4.5 inches (11.4cm)

Interestingly, the smaller varieties come near to the size of the original wild varieties. In the case of the Gloster this differs from natural canaries by its shape and sound colouring and, in the case of the **Corona,** by its crest.

DEVELOPMENT

Unlike the earlier varieties the Gloster has a well *recorded* history. It was first shown at the Crystal Palace Show of 1925 and is believed to be the result of crosses between three varieties:

1. **Crested**
2. **Border**
3. **Roller**

The smallest birds of these varieties were used to produce the first specimens of the Gloster and from then on careful breeding has resulted in the beautiful birds seen today.

Personalities involved

The personalities involved in the early efforts to create the breed were:

1. **Mrs Rogerson** of Cheltenham, Gloucestershire (from where the name was derived — a phonetic rendering of Gloucester) who showed the first Glosters as 'Crested'.

2. **John McLay** of Scotland who bred Glosters from Crested and Borders.

3. **A. W. Smith** of London who as a leading canary breeder and judge who led the movement to establish the new breed. He

wrote a book *The Gloster Fancy Canary* explaining the background and nature of the breed.

4. **John Robson** who finally accepted the new breed and by his influence (he was a leading judge) he increased their popularity.

Through their efforts and those of other enthusiasts in the Fancy the breed went from strength to strength. Today's fanciers carry on the tradition turning out excellent specimens which are able to compete successfully with the other, older breeds.

A.W. Smith, (*ibid*), reported that at the 1925 Palace Show Mr John McLay the judge asked his opinion on two small crested birds. He stated Mr McLay "was holding a couple of show cages in which were two of the smallest Crested canaries I had ever seen". A full report of that historic meeting is recorded in *The Gloster Fancy Canary* by A.W. Smith and is reproduced below:

EVOLUTION OF NAME

For my part, I coined the name Gloster Fancy Canary, appropriately to the district in which this lady pioneer was domiciled. I compiled its first Standard of Excellence, which, in essentials, still holds today. I sent particulars promptly to *Cage Birds*, and the variety has been known as the Gloster Fancy ever since.

How well John McLay fulfilled his promise to help may be gathered from the fact that he became the first President of the Gloster Fancy Canary Club, and he bred many sparkling gems, not forgetting a few scintillating Whites with blue head adornments; beautiful exhibits that captivated all who ever saw them. John certainly got the Glosters started in Scotland, but progress was slow, the Scottish fanciers were so conservative.

What surprised, and to some extent dismayed me, was that John Robson, the leading judge of those days, should at first rather condemn the variety with only faint praise. However, a little later on, when returning with him from a Reading show, in company with Mr. and Mrs. Shepherd, Mr. Wallington, and Mr. McLay, all renowned Crest breeders, a change came about in John Robson's views.

Apropos of nothing, so it seemed, or perhaps it was just a sly dig at Mr. McLay and myself in such a strong Crest atmosphere, he disparagingly remarked, "Glosters! Tut, tut!"

John McLay's ready retort was: "Aye, John! and you couldn't wish for better birds. They breed well, they are grand 'doers' and I like them immensely. What is more, I get ten inquiries for Glosters to one for Crests. How about that?"

This coming from a widely acknowledged celebrity in the Norwich and Crested varieties was testimony indeed, and Robbie, as he was affectionately known to us all, then generously conceded that we really had something well worthy of cultivation by our Canary breeders.

His backing was welcome because, of itself, it meant commendation of the new variety to all.

THE DESCRIPTION

Gloster canaries come in two main types:

1. Consort (or Plain Headed or Non-crested)
2. Corona (or Crested)

Either type can be a cock or hen. Despite the name 'consort' this does not imply a male, but rather a partner which will breed without complications.

Because Crest to Crest is a lethal gene in a double dose it follows that this harmony cross (Consort x Corona) is used each time.

Moreover the aim should be to produce well balanced crests which possess an even spread of feathers radiating from a centre point. This can only be achieved by following the Consort x Corona rule and by using well-shaped specimens of sound colour and without faults.

HISTORY OF THE CRESTED

Crested canaries have been around a long time. Indeed they were included in a list of existing canaries in the eighteenth century written by a Frenchman named Hervieux. At this stage writers on canaries suggest that the Crested was a 'sport" which occurred haphazardly.

Then the Lancashire Coppy and Norwich Crested appeared and reached a very high standard. In fact, the Norwich Crested was called the "King of the Fancy" with prices of more than £100 being paid and even £150 was paid for a single bird (and this was around 1920).

According to C. A. House (*Canaries & Cage Birds*, 1923) , it was in 1888 that classes were provided for Crest-bred birds. At that time the classes available (Crystal Palace) were:

Clear, Ticked, or Lightly Marked Yellow (13); Heavily Marked, Variegated or Green Yellow (16); Clear, Ticked, or Lightly Marked Buff (33); Heavily Marked, variegated, or Green Buff (18); Any Variety Yellow Hen (15); Any Variety Buff Hen (21); The late Joe Bexson, of Derby, was the Judge. From thence onward Crest-bred classes have been provided. At the same show, the Crest classes were evenly marked Yellow (12); Evenly marked Buff (20); Ticked Yellow (17); Ticked Buff (26); Clear Body Yellow (11); Clear-Body Dark Crested Buff (14); Clear-Body Light Crest Buff (13).

Two factors apparently caused their decline:

1. The high prices charged for birds which many fanciers could not afford. (Breeders must be more sensible for scarce breeds)

2. The crossing of the Norwich to get "improvements" which caused great controversy and a turning away from the Crested canary. The cross was with the Lancashire canary which resulted in a larger crested bird, but with a loss of feather quality, colour and shape.

An Early Crested Canary — note the large crest

Modern Crested Canary (still around 6½ ins. long)

The end result was a very large Crested type approaching eight inches in length. The body was equally massive with body and neck short and thick — a Bullfinch-type bird on a large scale. Dr. Karl Russ writing in the early part of this century, comparing the Norwich with the Hartz (Roller) canary stated "its build is somewhat more strong and thick-set, and it is rather larger".

That Victorian expert Claude St. John in *Our Canaries* recognized the Lancashire Coppy cross, but was not as disapproving as some writers. He stated: "The massive Crests of today are largely the result of a *wise intermix* (own italics) with the Lancashire Coppy".

The point which is being laboured is that for a considerable period, although criticized by fanciers, the tendency was for Crested birds to get larger and coarser. For this reason, when the Gloster came on the scene in 1925, it seemed that the impossible was being attempted — a Crested canary which was small and graceful. The *standard* for the Gloster states that the size must tend towards the **diminutive**.

Those early breeders set themselves a formidable task in trying to achieve the perfect circular crest and the small size now required. Indeed, from Claude St. John's statement quoted above, the very large Lancashire canaries produced the improved crest, and the new breed required.

COMPARISON WITH THE CRESTED

Illustrations of the Crested are shown in Figures 13-3/4. It will be seen that whilst the overall conformation may appear very similar there are marked differences. It is a large bird, around 6½ inches long, which originally had a large drooping crest covering the eyes. The Gloster is a small, refined bird with a perfectly formed crest.

14

THE GLOSTER
EXPLAINED

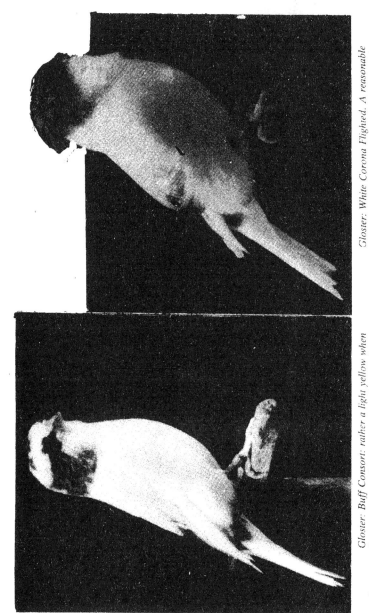

Gloster: White Corona Flighed. A reasonable specimen, but rather "feathery" and not compact enough (Photo: Ron and Val Moat)

Gloster: Buff Consort: rather a light yellow when shown up white on a monochrome print. A cobby specimen, but too upright (Photo: Ron and Val Moat)

Figure 14-3 Coarse and oversize Gloster

Roach Backed

Hollow Backed

Too narrow at front and wide at back

Shape Faults in Gloster

Loose and straggly

Too large

Broken Crest

Covering eyes

Crest Faults on Corona

THE CARDINAL FEATURES

A. W. Smith compiled the first *standard* for the breed. It is, therefore, appropriate to list the features he regarded as being of vital importance. Indeed the *standard* has varied very little from those early days.

1. **Glosters must be small birds.**
   Diminutive is the key word used by Gloster fanciers. "The Gloster is the Tom Thumb of the canary world" (A.W. Smith). The recommended size of not more than 4½ inches in length indicates that the smaller the better should be the aim.

2. **Type and Quality Must be Present**
   Breeding tiny birds that do not have a full rounded body or excellent feathering will lead to failure. By "type" is meant a full-rounded, cobby body with smooth lines.

   The ideal shape is elliptical; i.e., cone shaped with rounded ends. However, oval or egg shaped is also acceptable, but what A. W. Smith calls a "shield shape" narrow at the *front* and wide at the back is definitely unacceptable.

3. **The Corona or Crest**
   The crest should be neat and regular without any breaks in the round cap. There should be a small neat centre around which the crest is formed in an even manner. Moreover, the crest should not be loose or straggly, nor should it fall over the eyes so that the bird has difficulty in seeing. It follows that the eye should be discernible.

4. **The Head and Beak**
   Heads should be proportional to the body and features to **avoid** are:

   (a) wide skulls;
   (b) receding foreheads;
   (c) coarseness;
   (d) flat heads.

   The beak should be neat with small and neat mandibles; any coarseness spoils the head completely. In other words, aim for as small and fine a beak as possible in proportion to the head.

   The Consort head is of vital importance in breeding Coronas and Consorts. Remember the perfect head should be present for both and it can be seen most clearly on the Consort cock or hen.

Flat head

Receding forehead

Wide skull

Figure 14-6 Head Faults on Consort

Coarse Head and Beak on Consort

Thick clumsy legs

Long shanks

Long thighs

Short dumpy legs

Faulty legs on Gloster

Furthermore, the sulky appearance, fashionable at one time, should not be present because this trait follows crest-breeding and not true Gloster-breeding.

5. **Legs and Body**
Legs should be fine and of medium length with very little of the thigh showing. They should follow the natural lines of the body appearing to fit about two-thirds of the way along the body (from the head). This gives the bird a sprightly appearance —"that captivating light, quick, fairy-like action of the well-bred Gloster." Faults to **avoid** are:

(a) thick, clumsy legs;
(b) long shanks giving a stilty carriage;
(c) short, dumpy legs.

All these conflict with the sprightly requirements of this diminutive bird.

The **back** should contain no defects and should be nicely rounded to fit into the overall conformation of the body. At the same time, viewed sideways, the back should be straight, without the curve known as roach-backed, an indication of coarseness. A hollow back is also a serious fault.

On the general roundness of the body the positioning of the **wings** is of vital importance. They should fit closely to the body with primary tips meeting in a point at the base of the tail. The shoulders should be smooth and round and not too pronounced or the harmony of the "wings well laid on" is not achieved.

Faults to **avoid** with the wings are:

(a) too long;
(b) cross-feathered or loose;
(c) split-winged.

The **tail** is of equal importance because this gives the balance and harmony required by the *standard*. It should follow the natural lengthening of the bird, being in a straight line from the end of the back, with a narrow base and closely fitting feathers, tightly folded, forming an integral and neat finish to the overall shape. Faults which should be penalised are:

(a) a lifted tail like a Robin;
(b) a droopy tail;
(c) loose or broken feathers.

Dropped Wings

Crossed Wings

Figure 14-9 Wing Faults on Gloster

Lifted Tail (Robin)

Droopy Tail

Loose or broken feathers

Tail Faults on Gloster

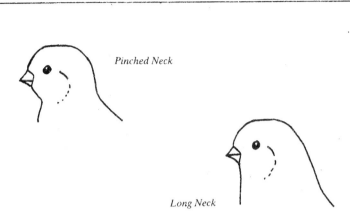

Pinched Neck

Long Neck

Figure 14-11 Neck Faults on Gloster

Ideal Neck and Rounded Body

The roundness of the body has already been stressed. This is essential and according to the *standard* it should be nicely rounded without due prominence. In the diagram issued by A.W. Smith the head, neck and body are most certainly not pronounced. There is clear evidence of a bird with gentle curves with no point exaggerated. Since those days there has been a change in the overall shape; the head is larger and the neck is shorter; the body is rounder with a more positive cobby appearance.

The original diagram showing the ideal bird envisaged by Mr. Smith is shown overleaf. If this is compared with the modern *standards* the changes which have taken place over a period of half a century can be seen. Such an evolution is inevitable and it has occurred with most breeds of canary, the Lizard, being the main exception. As judges express their views and award places in shows on *their* interpretation of the *standards* so the type of bird being bred is gradually modified.

The **neck** should be in harmony with the body; it should be *full*. Precisely what is meant by "full" is not clear. As noted earlier there is now a more definite bull-neck which in turn affects the overall impression.

6. **Plumage**
The plumage should be of a high quality with a tight silky appearance; what the poultry fancier calls "hard feathered". Excess fluff or feathers should not be present because these would detract from the smooth lines expected from this miniature canary.

Many people confuse the Gloster with the Crested, but this should not be the case. Besides being a much larger bird (around 6½ inches) the Crested has a large, round and drooping crest — the larger the better. Moreover, the feathering is profuse and wings much longer than those on the Gloster.

THE STANDARDS

When judging Glosters it is usual to follow the *standard* and award points on the basis of the ideal with deductions for any defects. Both fanciers and would-be judges must know the standards for the breed being kept.

In the case of Glosters the standards of excellence are controlled by the Gloster Canary Convention which has around 24 specialist societies.

FIRST IDEAL OF GLOSTER

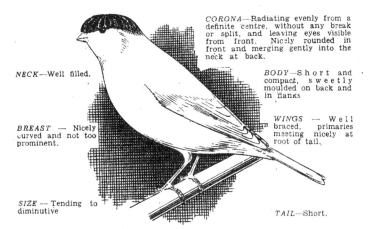

CORONA—Radiating evenly from a definite centre, without any break or split, and leaving eyes visible from front. Nicely rounded in front and merging gently into the neck at back.

NECK—Well filled.

BODY—Short and compact, sweetly moulded on back and in flanks

BREAST — Nicely curved and not too prominent.

WINGS — Well braced, primaries meeting nicely at root of tail.

SIZE — Tending to diminutive

TAIL—Short.

Diagram depicting the show points of a Gloster.

NB. This is now superseded.

The early model as developed by A.W. Smith and other Pioneers

There is a description for the Corona and another for the Consort and this is supplemented by a *Pictorial Standard drawn by Charles Minjoodt and adopted by the Gloster Canary Convention.*

The original standard still stands as a monument to A.W. Smith and other fanciers who drafted the first descriptions.

Modern Type of Consort.

Leaning over perch

Stance Fault

Too upright

Faults in Stance (Correct Angle 45°).

15

THE MODERN GLOSTER

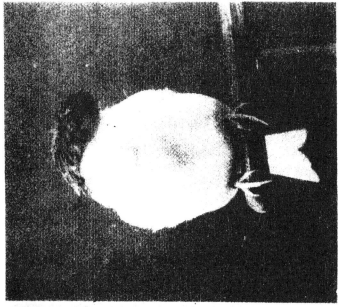

Figure 15-1 Front view of Buff Dark Crest Corona. A well-shaped front and reasonable crest (needs straightening)

(Photo: Ron and Val Moat)

Figure 15-2 Side view of Buff Consort. A compact, cobby bird. but a little too fluffy around thighs.

(Photo: Ron and Val Moat)

PROGRESS IN THE FANCY

The active societies have encouraged members to develop the Gloster so that top class birds have developed a shape and character all of their own. They require to be shapely with a tendency to be cobby; i.e., short and rounded. In addition, they have to be healthy, agile, alert and constantly on the move.

As a result of the careful selection and breeding which has taken place birds which comply with the *standard* are seen quite regularly, but there are still many which do not achieve the desired level of excellence. An analysis of some of the major faults still seen is therefore appropriate to guide the fancier on what he is trying to achieve with modern birds:

1. **Size**
    This is a controversial area the ideal being a *maximum* of 4¼ inches. Some fanciers have suggested that 4¼ inches would be more in keeping with the term *diminutive*. In practice, under inexperienced judges, much larger birds have been given prizes. They are cobby and comply with the *standard* in all respects except for size. Such cage birds should not be awarded top honours at any show. Mr. Cliff Harris a National Exhibition judge expressed his opinion for the 1986 show in that he stated he would be "seeking examples of the most diminutive exhibits* he could find. The size is not specified in the *standards*, but obviously over-size is a very serious fault. Mr. Harris felt that a length of 4¼ inches (10.5cm) would be ideal.

2. **Corona and Head on Consort**
    The corona, cap or crest should be neat and regular with a clearly defined centre. Many fail because of faults such as irregular length or shape of features. Frontal feathers may be too long extending beyond the base of the beak. Sometimes the eyes are masked by the corona. Bald spots are another blemish which call for a penalty. The existence of short frontal feathers is also a serious fault and "tufts" and "horns" should not be present.

    The perfect corona is awarded 20 points including 5 for the definite centre. Accordingly, a faulty crest should keep any Corona from the top awards.

    The Consort should have a broad head, but as A.W. Smith specified many years ago this should be in proportion to the ideal sized body. Excessive broadness probably means over-sized

---

* Reported in *Cage and Aviary Birds*, 6th December, 1986 page 5, John Emslie

Figure 15-3 Three-parts Dark Corona. A poor specimen with excess feathering, weak chest and untidy crest.

(Photo: Ron and Val Moat)

Figure 15-4 Side view of three-parts Dark Corona. Gives better impression, but body too long and thin

(Photo: Ron and Val Moat)

bodies and coarseness. The eyebrow should be "heavy" but apparently not too "browy"*.

Again, 20 points are awarded for these features.

3. **Neck and Breast**

A common fault is the neck being too "dipped in" with the result that both the back and front show a break which is not conducive to the smooth lines required. The early Glosters portrayed this fault as shown by the diagram contained in A.W. Smith's *The Gloster Fancy Canary* (See Figure 14-13).

4. **The Tail**

The tail set at the wrong angle such as the Robin-tail has already been mentioned. The drawing earlier (Figure 14-10) shows what is meant by this term and is self-explanatory.

5. **Plumage**

Many birds fail at shows because they are out of condition and the plumage shows this fact! Lack of sheen, broken feathers, evidence of mite and an overall impression of being ruffled are all examples of departure from the clear-cut lines made up of perfect feathers.

Presentation is vital because a sound bird will be at a definite advantage when properly groomed, whereas without the effort of spraying and other requirements (see Chapter 10) the overall impression will be unfavourable.

SEXUAL DIFFERENCES

When a canary carries the tag of "diminutive" it follows that there will be controversy on what is the ideal size and when are birds too big. Usually the cock bird tends to be more bulky than the hen and therefore he may be penalised for being too large. Moreover, hens may have better colouring than cocks which also gives them an advantage.

This sexual difference is not allowed in the *standards*, unlike the poultry fancy where the difference in size is specified in definite terms.

CONCLUSIONS

The *standards* show what consitutes Ideal Gloster Fancy Canary. They may be interpreted in different ways by individual judges and

---

* **Cliff Harris**, *ibid.*

breeders; over the years changes have taken place in the birds bred to conform with the ideals laid down. Nevertheless, the aim must be to achieve even better quality and breeders and exhibitors will continue to aim for perfection. There should be no departure from the basic requirements explained.

Hand Feeding.

The instrument here shown is a very useful addition to the breeders' equipment.

16

COLOURS IN GLOSTERS

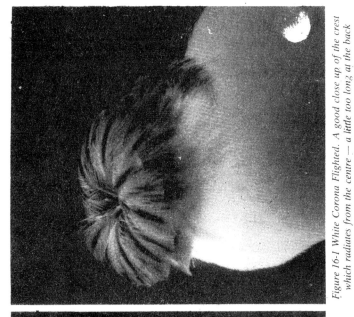

Figure 16-1 White Corona Flighted. A good close up of the crest which radiates from the centre — a little too long at the back

(Photo: Ron and Val Moat)

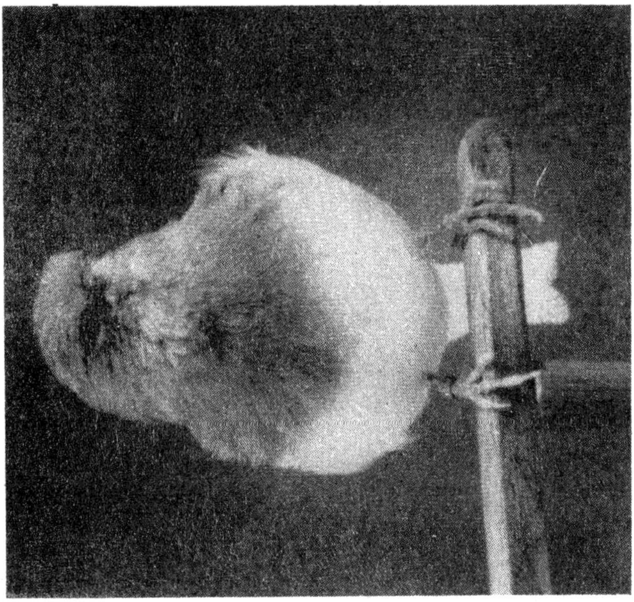

Figure 16-2 Buff Consort. Front view of a full-breasted Gloster

(Photo: Ron and Val Moat)

BASIC COLOURS

The wild canary is a relatively plain bird when compared with his domesticated counterpart. Their natural colour "is a greyish brown merging into yellowish green in the underparts of the body".* In fact, this description varies a little from some given but it suffices to show that the wild bird resembles many other species of bird and in fact in size is rather like a Linnet.

Basically there are two colours in the domesticated canary:

1. Yellow
2. Buff (Fanciers prefer to call this "Mealy")

The main difference between these two is in the pigmentation in the feathers. When the lipochrome is present to a marked degree the positive yellow is created. If it is weak then the "buff" colour appears, the absence of yellow colouring bringing in a lighter, mealy colour.

CLEARS AND VARIATIONS

If birds have one basic colour they are "clears". Superimposed upon a clear bird may be various patterns or features. Thus a canary may be variegated or it may have a dark crest and these variations must be described; thus:

Dark Crested Yellow Corona Cock, — depicting a clear bird with the exception of the crest.

A "Self" bird is one which has the same colour throughout without any light feathers in the plumage. Usually the description is applied to Greens and Cinnamons.

ADDITIONAL COLOURS

From the basic yellow came other colours and no doubt others will follow. They include:

1. **Greens**
2. **Cinnamons**
3. **Variegated**
4. **White**
5. **Blue**
6. **Fawn**

In addition, there are variations of these colours. Indeed, some of the descriptions become quite complicated such as: "A flighted three-parts

* *The Canary* Its Varieties, Management and Breeding, Rev. F. Smith, c 1890

Buff Consort. (Photo: Ron and Val Moat)
A small bird, but could be faulted as follows.
   (a) *Possibly a little too browy*
   (b) *Upright (instead of 45°)*
   (c) *Lacking full rounded breast*
   (d) *Body long and thin.*
   (e) *Although "proportioned" not ideal*
   (f) *Too feathery*

Dark Green Buff Corona cock" a bird recently illustrated in *Cage and Aviary Birds*. The fancier will learn to distinguish the difficult colours by going to shows and discussing them with experienced exhibitors.

BREEDING FOR COLOURS

Double Buffing

That pioneer of the Gloster Fancy, A.W. Smith believed that buff to buff was an essential requirement for maintaining strong colours and he called this process "double buffing". This is a practice still followed except periodically (again recommended by Smith) a yellow is introduced to keep the positive colour. Once every four or five years appears to be the vogue, but there is clearly a need for experiment in this area because a dark crested brightly coloured bird is a very desirable exhibit.

There are two features which should be watched when double buffing takes place:

1. Tightness and quality of feather;
2. Size and shape of crest.

Introducing the yellow strengthens the quality of the feathers giving it back the lustre which is so desirable. In addition, carefully selected the yellow may be used to improve the crest.

Another feature to watch is the texture of the feathers and the fluffy appearance which may appear around the thighs and vent which damages the smooth appearance so essential in a top quality bird.

Because of the concentration on Buffs the Yellows do not always come up to the ideal, cobby shape. Accordingly, they have to be selected with care. In any event, the shape may require improving once the yellow injection has taken place.

GREENS

The wild canary has three basic colours yellow, black and brown. In the absence of black and brown the yellow appears, but taken together there are different variations of green.

Since the plumage on a dark bird tends to be very glossy it follows that greens are excellent partners in a breeding programme.

Three-Parts Green Glosters

Reference has been made to a "three-parts dark green" bird, earlier in this chapter. This technical term is used to denote that three quarters is dark whereas one-quarter is light. This lightness may be in any part of the body, but if in excess of one-quarter it becomes a variegated bird.

This variegation may appear on any part of the body, but is usually on the wings and so does little damage when used for breeding.

Undoubtedly, Greens produce the depth and richness of colour required for a top-class Gloster. If a variegated Green Consort is used as one partner with careful selection any unwanted head markings can be avoided.

VARIEGATED

This applies to birds which have a mixture of colours in an uneven pattern. Provided their background is known they can be used for breeding purposes; i.e., whether Green-bred or Cinnamon bred. A.W. Smith regards birds with high variegation (not mousey!) as a means of improving the plumage.

WHITES

Whites produced from Buffs will rarely produce pure white birds. This is because the yellow colour continues to tinge the white. For Glosters the **dominant** white is the type produced.

The practical way to produce the pure white bird is by careful selection after breeding as follows:

Small white hen **well-shaped and** **close feathered**	x	**Yellow cock** **well-shaped**

Select white females with desired qualities and breed with Buff cocks.

Again select for closeness of feather, size, shape and other requirements, including the corona.

The process is repeated until the much improved White is produced.

This was the system advocated by A.W. Smith. It will be noticed that he advocated using a Yellow cock. Many breeders would not agree with this approach and would prefer Buff to White, the Yellow being regarded as too strong a colour for getting the good White colour.

The fact remains that Dominant White mated to a Dominant White is not successful because 25 per cent would have a lethal gene. The balance would be 50 per cent Dominant White and 25 per cent Normal. Obviously, like all statistics, a sufficient number would have to be bred for the *tendencies* to prove correct.

SCIENTIFIC BASIS FOR COLOUR SELECTIONS

The introduction of a new colour into the double-buffing method of breeding has been stressed. Without an influx of the strengthening colour the plumage deteriorates and Self with Self results in a loss of the buff colour.

An understanding of the process involved should enable the breeder to work out for himself why colours occur as they do. Following a period of speculation on how colours were formed discoveries showed that pigments produce the colour.

As noted earlier there are two basic pigments:

1. Lipochrome
2. Melanin

The lipochrome pigments in feathers provide the brightest feathers of all. Unfortunately, they are affected by environmental factors, particularly the diet fed to canaries. It means that an unbalanced diet can result in loss of colour and feather condition. In the canary the yellow colour is provided by the lipochrome pigment.

Melanins provide the feathers with black and reddish-brown colours. They are in the vane of the feather in granules. The existence of these granules provide the appropriate level of colour.

The presence of melanin results in the feathers accumulating a chemical which helps to keep them longer than when the pigment is not present. This greater resilience, which it gives to the feathers, should be used to advantage in the breeding programme. This is why the darker birds such as green and cinnamon deepen and bring back the sheen. In fact, metallic sheen exists only when pigment is present to a marked degree.

White feathers have little or no pigment and that is why they do not possess a brilliant sheen. It follows that variegated or grizzled birds have pigment which is diffused throughout the feather structure; the light parts indicate the absence of pigment.